Published by Sourcebooks eXplore, an imprint of Sourcebooks Kids

P.O. Box 4410, Naperville, Illinois 60567–4410

(630) 961-3900

sourcebookskids.com

First published as Red Kangaroo's Thousands Physics Whys: *The World Is Made Up of Atoms*
in 2018 in China by China Children's Press and Publication Group.

Library of Congress Cataloging-in-Publication Data is on file with the publisher.

Source of Production: PrintPlus Limited, Shenzhen, Guangdong Province, China

Date of Production: August 2020

Run Number: 5018839

Printed and bound in China.

PP 10 9 8 7 6 5 4 3 2 1

Let's Get Tiny!

Jumping into the Science of the Smallest Part of Matter with Quantum Physics

sourcebooks
eXplore

**#1 Bestselling
Science Author for Kids
Chris Ferrie**

Red Kangaroo is outside with Dr. Chris, trying out her new magnifying glass.

"When I look through this, I can see the small patterns on this butterfly's wings and the tiny parts of this flower," Red Kangaroo says. "But what are these things made of?"

"Great question, Red Kangaroo," Dr. Chris says. "Let's go to the lab."

"Dr. Chris," says Red Kangaroo. "What are a butterfly's wings and a flower's petals made of?"

"Everything in the world is made up of very, very small things called atoms." Dr. Chris says. "Butterflies, flowers, even you and I are made of atoms."

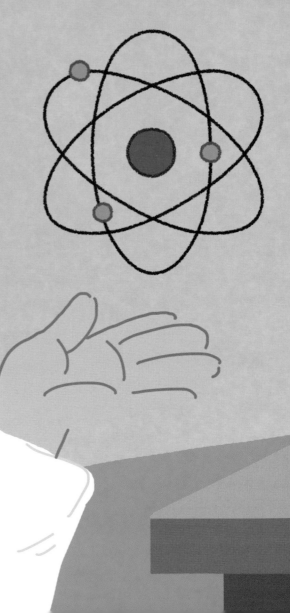

"Wow!" says Red Kangaroo. "But what is an atom?"

"Atoms are kind of like toy blocks or like bricks that builders use. They're small on their own but you can put many of them together to create something much bigger. Atoms are the building blocks that make up everything we see around us—this apple, that caterpillar, this ball, and that plane. These things may look pretty different, but they're all made of atoms!" Dr. Chris says.

"So everything is made of atoms," says Red Kangaroo. "But what are atoms made of?"

"Another great question! An **atom** is made of even smaller things! An atom has three parts: electrons, protons, and neutrons," says Dr. Chris. "But the world of the atom is far too small to see with our eyes!"

"This is a diagram of an atom," explains Dr. Chris. "Scientists often use diagrams to think about and explain things that we cannot see, hear, or feel."

"In the middle of the diagram is the atomic **nucleus**, made up of **protons** and **neutrons**," Dr. Chris explains. "And on the outside, **electrons** orbit the nucleus like kids running around their parents."

"What are the different circles for, Dr. Chris?" Red Kangaroo asks.

"The circles are called **orbits**," says Dr Chris. "The orbits show us where the electrons can be and how much energy they can have."

"Electrons in each orbit have different **energy**. Electrons have the most energy at the outermost orbit and the least energy at the innermost orbit," explains Dr Chris. "But the most important thing is that the electrons never visit the space between the orbits!"

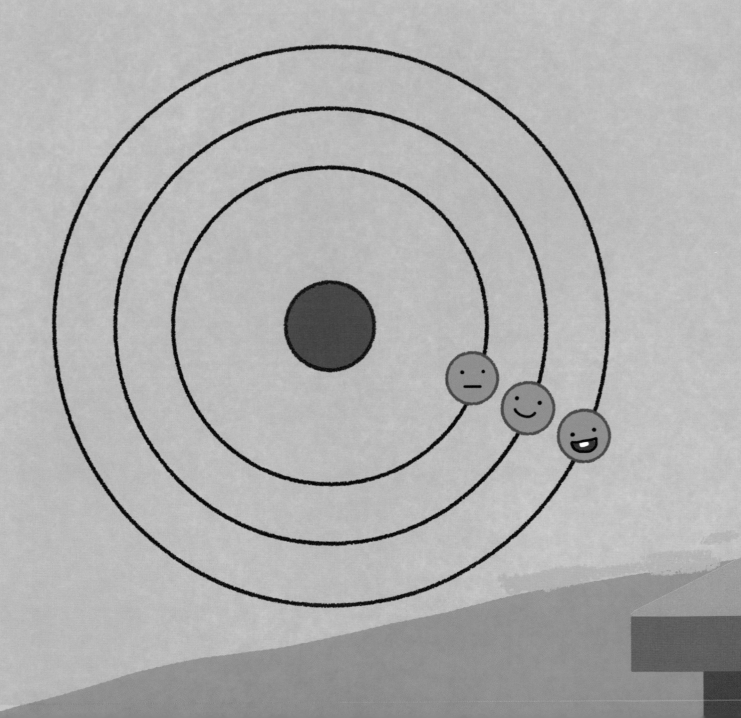

"But how can the energy change without the electron visiting the space between?" Red Kangaroo asks, scratching her head.

"Another great question!" says Dr. Chris. "Let's follow these tricky electrons."

"When an electron changes energy, it jumps from one orbit to another," says Dr. Chris. "Can you imagine being an electron like this, Red Kangaroo?"

"I know!" says Red Kangaroo "I can be like an electron by using stairs instead of a slide to go from a high place to a low place. Right, Dr. Chris?"

"Exactly!" says Dr. Chris. "You are moving from step to step just like an electron."

"When an electron jumps between orbits, its energy changes," Dr. Chris says. "To jump outward, the electron takes on more energy. To jump inward, the electron gives away energy."

"I need energy too, just like the electron!" says Red Kangaroo. "I use up my energy as I jump toward home. Then I get energy with my food and jump away to play again!"

"When the electron jumps up or down between orbits, it takes or gives a little bit of energy one step at a time." Dr Chris explains. "That little bit of energy is called a quantum. Now you are a quantum physicist!"

"Oh yes!" exclaims Red Kangaroo, "Now I know that everything is made of atoms and how the atom's energy works! Thanks for teaching me about **quantum physics**, Dr. Chris!"

Glossary

Atom
The building blocks that make up everything around us, including the elements.

Nucleus
The central part of the atom containing protons and neutrons.

Proton
A positively charged particle within the nucleus of an atom.

Quantum Physics
A branch of science which studies the relationship between matter and energy at the smallest scale.

Neutron
An uncharged particle within the nucleus of an atom.

Electron

A negatively charged particle that orbits the nucleus of an atom.

Orbit

Regular movement around an object.

Energy

A property of things that allows them to move and do work.

Show What You Know

1. What are the building blocks of all things?

2. Name the central part of an atom.

3. Name the small particles that orbit the nucleus of an atom.

4. When Red Kangaroo imagined being an electron, what example did she use to understand how electrons change energy?

5. What does an electron do to move between orbits?

Test It Out

What glows in the night

1. You will need a flashlight, glow-in-the-dark stickers or clothing, and a UV light. You can find UV flashlights at the pet store (to find pee-pee spots on the carpet—gross!) or use "spy pens" that write invisible ink.

2. In a dark room, shine the flashlight and UV light on different glow-in-the-dark stickers. (It works better if the light from one flashlight doesn't hit the other.)

3. Turn the lights off at the same time and record your observations. Did the stickers glow the same under both lights?

4. What can you deduce about the energy of the lights from how bright the stickers glow?

5. If you have different color lights (LED flashlights are different than incandescent bulbs, for example), try the experiment again. Which light do you think has the highest energy?

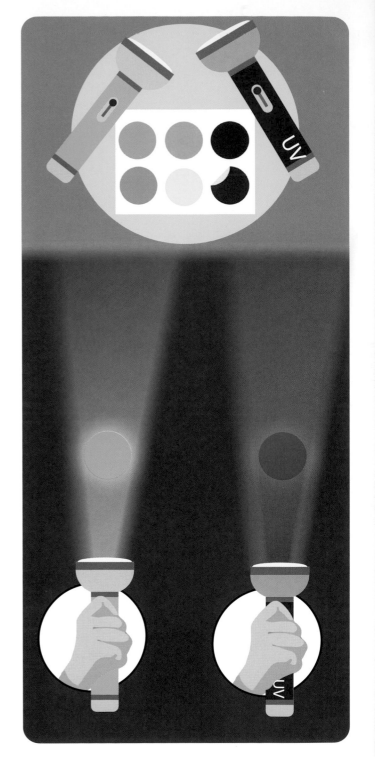

What glows in the light

1. You will need white paper, markers, highlighters, and a UV light. You can find UV flashlights at the pet store or use "spy pens" that write invisible ink.

2. On a blank piece of paper, draw and color in some one-inch diameter dots with each color marker and highlighter.

3. Shine the UV light on the dots. Record what you see.

4. Turn the UV light back off and record what you see now. Is there a difference?

5. Does the same thing happen when you use a regular flashlight, light bulb, or even sunshine?

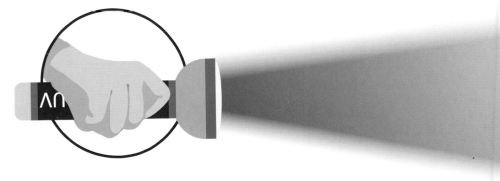

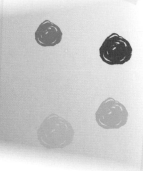

What to expect when you Test it Out

What glows in the night

   Glow-in-the-dark stickers are phosphorescent, which means the electrons in the atoms jump up to higher energy levels and slowly fall down to lower energy levels, letting out different colored light. The more energy the light has, the higher the energy of the electrons will be and the more light you will see in the dark. Even though light from a UV flashlight doesn't seem as bright to our eyes, the energy of UV light is higher than the colors our eyes can see, so UV light gives the electrons the most energy. No matter how bright the regular flashlight is, its energy will never match that of UV light.

What glows in the light

   Unlike glow-in-the-dark stickers, the ink in highlighters is not phosphorescent, but fluorescent. This means that the electrons do not store energy and do not slowly jump down. When you turn off the UV light, the highlighter stops glowing immediately. The highlighter does not glow in white light because the energy levels the electrons must reach are too high—there is not enough energy in the light of a regular flashlight. The energy of UV light is just right for the electrons to jump up, but they immediately fall back down and release light of different colors.

Show What You Know answers

1. All things are built up of atoms.

2. The central part of an atom is called the nucleus.

3. Electrons orbit the nucleus.